PUSS JUNIOR AND ROBINSON CRUSOE

INSIGHT PUBLICA®

AF516885

Nadakkavu, Kozhikode, Kerala, 673011
www.insightpublica.com
e-mail: insightpublica@gmail.com
Title: **PUSS JUNIOR AND ROBINSON CRUSOE**
Author: **DAVID CORY**
First Insight Edition: May 2025
Printed and Published by
InsightinPublica Printers & Publishers Pvt. Ltd.
ISBN: 978-93-5517-850-3
₹ 180

PUSS JUNIOR AND ROBINSON CRUSOE

DAVID CORY

INSIGHT PUBLICA®

CONTENTS

JACK SPRAT

ONE day as little Puss, Junior, was traveling through New Mother Goose country, he came to a funny little house all covered with rose vines, even up to the top of the small red chimney they grew in crimson splendor. And as Puss stopped to look at the pretty sight, a tiny blue bird in a cage on the front porch began to sing:

"Jack Sprat had a pig,
Who was not very big;
He was not very lean
He was not very fat;
'He'll do for a grunt,'
Says little Jack Sprat."

"Oh, ho," thought Puss, and he turned into the yard and walked around to the little red barn. There stood Jack Sprat himself, leaning against the sty, watching his pig eat his dinner.

Well, just then, all of a sudden, a swarm of golden bees came humming into the little farmyard, and before long they had made a home in the empty beehive that stood close by.

"You have brought me luck," said little Jack Sprat, turning to Puss. "Now I shall have honey, and with bees and a pig I shall grow rich and supply all Mother Goose Country with good things to eat." And would you believe it, the pig began to grow fat, and the bees to buzz out of the hive and wing their way over to the roses for sweets with which to make their honey.

Then Jack Sprat asked Puss to come into his little house, and when he went to the cupboard to look for bread and butter, he found all kinds of good things to eat.

"What luck you have brought me," said little Jack Sprat,

but Puss was as much surprised as he. But pretty soon when they had sat down to the table, they heard a strange little voice from the hearth, and looking down they saw a tiny black cricket, who began to sing:

"I'm just a little cricket,

But if you'll let me stay

Within your house this winter

You will not rue the day."

"It is the little cricket that brings you luck," said truthful little Puss, Junior. And then Jack Sprat began to laugh happily, for up to this time the pig was the only thing he owned, and that wasn't very much, let me tell you. Oh, dear, no. Not in these hard times when eggs are worth their weight in gold and a gallon of milk costs a ton of silver.

Well, by and by, Puss, Junior, once more went on his way, and perhaps pretty soon he'll find his father, the famous Puss in Boots, unless,

A great big husky giant

Jumps into a trolley car,

And turns the coin box upside down

To see how many nickels there are.

THE YELLOW HEN

WELL, a big husky giant didn't jump into the trolley car, as I feared he might in the last story, so little Puss, Junior, kept up his search for his dear father until late in the evening when he came to a city on Goosey Gander River. For the moment I've forgotten the name, but if I remember it I will tell you later. At any rate, it won't matter much, for Puss didn't stay there long. Well, as I was saying, he entered the city, tired and hungry, for he had traveled far that day, and as he walked up the brightly lighted street he heard a man say:

"Saw ye aught of my love a-coming from the Opera?
Around her throat a string of pearls,
And on her neck two little curls;
Saw ye aught of my love a-coming from the Opera?

"My good man, I'm a stranger and have just arrived. I have seen no string of pearls nor little curls on any pretty little girls," answered Puss wearily, for he was too anxious to find a night's lodging to notice pearls and curls.

"Dear me!" sighed the man, and he took off his opera hat and flattened it and then snapped it out again, which made a little newsboy open his eyes and say, "Do it again, Mister;

it sounds like a pistol." But the man wouldn't, so the little newsboy ran off and Puss turned away, for he had no time to be talking to operagoers at that time of evening. By and by he came to a narrow street at the end of which shone a little light. So he turned down and presently found himself in front of a little house. In the hammock on the front porch sat a pretty yellow hen, swinging back and forth, and every now and then singing to herself:

"It's after ten! It's after ten!

Time for bed for Yellow Hen."

"Good evening!" said Puss, taking off his plumed hat and bowing politely. "May I ask for a night's lodging. I'm tired and footsore, and have traveled many miles in New Mother Goose Country."

The little Yellow Hen flapped her wings and fluttered down to the piazza. "Come," she said, stretching out her right wing. "Travelers are always welcome. We hear little down at the end of this narrow street. Tell me some news, my good Sir Cat."

"Are you sure you are not too sleepy?" asked Puss. "It was only a few minutes ago you were singing 'It's after ten, it's after ten; time for bed for Yellow Hen!'" But the little hen only laughed and said, "I must wait up for Mr. Rooster."

"He's the Cock at early dawn

Who blows on the Mayor's auto horn

To wake the city and stir the men

To be up and at their work again."

Just then a gaily feathered rooster walked up the steps, but what he said I shall have to tell you in the next story, for it's so late now that I must say good-night.

DICKORY DARE PIG

YOU remember, I hope, where I left off in the last story—just as the rooster came up the steps of the little house at the end of the narrow street where Puss, Junior, was making a call on the little Yellow Hen. Well, he was very much surprised to see our small traveler, but nevertheless he was most polite. He stretched forth his right wing to shake hands when, all of a sudden,

Dickory, dickory, dare,
The pig flew up the stair,
A very funny thing to do,
And made the rooster doodle-doo.

"Gracious me! Oh me, Oh my!" screamed the little Yellow Hen. "That awful pig will just spoil my stair carpet." This made the rooster all the more angry at the Dickory Dare Pig, as he called him, and he strutted across the piazza. "I'll spur him when he comes down," he said, and he waited at the front door. But Mr. Pig took no chances. He staid upstairs until the little Yellow Hen began to cry. "I want to go to bed." Puss, by this time, was also very sleepy, and the gaily feathered rooster—well, I think he was half asleep, as he stood by the front door, with his head tucked under his wing.

"He'll forget to crow in the early morn;
And little Boy Blue with his silver horn
Is always asleep, so what shall I do
If my Rooster sleeps the whole night through?"

"It's time for me to do something," exclaimed Puss, Junior, whipping out his sword and running upstairs two at a time. But, would you believe it if I told you, he couldn't find the Dickory Dare Pig anywhere? Puss looked in every room and in every closet. He even lifted the cover of the big clothes hamper that stood in the bathroom, but Mr. Pig was not to be found.

Well, after a while, Puss looked out of the window. There on the roof of the porch was the Dickory Dare Pig. "What are you doing?" asked Puss, and he waved his sword threateningly. But the Pig only grunted.

"You people downstairs are making an awful fuss," and he closed his eyes again, he was so sleepy. And, anyway, he had a very nice soft place, for he had spread a big woolen comforter on the roof for a bed.

"Well, you get out of here," said Puss. "You have no right to take the Yellow Hen's nice comforter, nor have you any right to sleep on the roof, and if you don't go I'll stick my sword in you." Well, after that, the Pig ran downstairs and out of the front door, and maybe he's running yet, if a butcher hasn't caught him and made him into little sausages.

THROUGH THE FOREST

YOU remember when we left off in the last story, Puss had just made the Dickory Dare Pig get off the roof of the Yellow Hen's front piazza, after which the gaily feathered rooster and the Yellow Hen and Puss, Junior, went to sleep, which they couldn't do before on account of that dreadful pig snoring. Well, he never came back, for he was so afraid of Puss, Junior's, sword, that he kept on running until he lost his shadow, spent a year and a day hunting for it, and after that he sat down and rested.

The next morning bright and early, just as the sun was waking up in the East, the gaily feathered Rooster began to blow his silver horn to wake the people before the morn, and some got cross when they heard his song, but others hurried their dressing along, and pretty soon Puss was dressed and the little Yellow Hen combed her feathers and came down to breakfast. And while they were at the table, the Rooster came in and said:

"There was an old woman, as I've heard tell,
Who went to market her eggs to sell.
As she went to market her eggs to sell
On the asphalt pavement she slipped and fell.

Then came a policeman whose name was Stout,
When he saw all the eggs lying strewn about,
He said, 'What is this, a river of eggs
Too bad, my old woman, you slipped on your legs!'
Then he helped the little old woman to stand,
And placing a new dollar bill in her hand,
He said, 'My old woman, don't scramble your eggs
On the pavement again by losing your legs.'"

"I'll never let her take my eggs to market," said the Yellow Hen, and the Rooster flapped his wings and crowed, he was so glad. And after that Puss, Junior, said good-by and went upon his journey, and by and by he came to a forest. Now this forest was full of bold robbers, but Puss didn't know that, so he walked in and by and by he came to a little hut. From the chimney a thin gray feather of smoke slowly made its way up through the tall tree tops, and around the front door climbed a wild vine. Puss went up boldly and knocked and when the door opened he saw a fox. At first he was somewhat frightened, but the fox said, "Come in, Sir Cat," so our little traveler entered and sat down.

Then the fox asked him where he was going. "To see my dear father, the famous Puss in Boots," replied little Puss, Junior. "It's not very far from here," answered the fox, "but the way is dangerous. Many robbers lie in wait for the unwary traveler."

"I have my trusty sword," cried Puss, "I'm not afraid."

"Well, since you are so brave, I will help you," said the fox; "I know a way and will show you how you may escape the robbers."

A TURTLE AND A FISH

AS I told you in the last story, the Fox promised to help Puss and pretty soon he led him out of the little log house and through a thick undergrowth of young timber until they came to a river. "Now, the robbers will never think for a moment that you would travel by water," said the Fox with a grin. "Here is a little boat," and he pushed aside the bushes behind which lay a rowboat with a pair of oars.

As Puss got in, the Fox gave him some parting directions. "Follow the stream until you come to a lake. Then leave your boat and follow the right bank until you come to a bridge. After that you will find the highway which will take you to the castle of my Lord of Carabas, where your famous father, Puss in Boots, lives."

"Thank you, my good friend," cried our little hero, pushing off from the shore, and in a few minutes he was gliding down the stream.

"Heigh-ho!" he sighed. "This is a new way to travel, but I have had many experiences, so why not a rowboat instead of a gander or an automobile," and he bent to his rowing and by and by he came to a bend in the river, and as it was late in the afternoon, he decided to land and camp for the night. But no sooner had he landed on the bank than a large turtle came up to him and said:

"This is Turtle Island. No one is allowed to land unless he has a permit." Of course, little Puss, Junior, didn't have one, but after a moment's reflection, he said:

"I am about to visit my father, the famous Puss in Boots, and if I cannot remain here for the night, I may have an accident on the river. Please let me stay."

"Very well," said the Turtle, scratching his head, "you may remain on my island," and then he crawled away to his own house on the hill, which Puss could see in the distance. I think the Turtle was a disagreeable sort of person not to have asked our little traveler to spend the night with him, but then, you know, there are some disagreeable people even in New Mother Goose Country, and the Turtle was one of them.

The next morning, bright and early, Puss, Junior, got up and cooked his breakfast, and then he jumped into his rowboat and started off and by and by, as he was gliding along, a big fish came up to the surface and said, "Helloa, there!" At first Puss was startled, for he didn't see the fish, but as soon as he did, he replied:

"Don't get in my way! I might push my oar in your eye." This made the fish laugh so hard that he cried, and after that he laughed some more, only he didn't cry that time. "Where are you going?" he asked.

"To the castle of my Lord of Carabas," replied Puss.

"A long journey, my brave little cat," said the fish, "but keep up a brave heart. You are already more than half way across New Mother Goose Country."

PUSS FINDS A SUPPER

FOR many days Puss, Junior, traveled in his boat down the river and towards evening he heard a voice on the shore singing:

"Rock-a-by baby, thy cradle is green,
Dad's a policeman, the finest yet seen;
And mother's a lady and goes to a ball,
And Johnny's a member of Tammany Hall."

Of course this made our little traveler laugh, for he didn't know there was a Tammany Hall in New Mother Goose Country and neither did I until Puss told me.

Well, he pulled his boat up on the bank and got out, and after that he listened again for the song, but there wasn't a sound, so he thought the baby must be asleep. Then he tiptoed over to a little cottage nearby and looked in the window. There sat a pretty little woman with a baby in her arms. And when she saw Puss she lifted her finger very gently to let him know that her baby was in the Land of Nod, and after that she placed him gently in the cradle.

"Come in," she whispered to our little pussy cat traveler and when they were in the nice bright kitchen, for the fire in the stove made bright streaks of light over the clean floor, she said:

"Sir Cat, you are a traveler, I see. Tell me one of your adventures while I get the supper. My good man will soon be home, hungry and tired from his day's work."

Now Puss, Junior, was tired, too, and he didn't feel a bit like sitting down and telling a story. But he was an obliging little pussy and he knew, like Little Tommy Tucker, he must pay for his supper.

"Once upon a time," he began, "there was a famous cat, and the reason he was so famous was because he had done a great favor for his master. You see, his master was the youngest of three sons, who, when his father died, got nothing but the cat, while the others got the farm and the money. But he never complained, which so pleased the cat that he made up his mind to help his young master. And what do you think he did? One day his master's clothes were stolen while in bathing, and the king, who was passing by at that moment in his coach, felt so sorry that he gave the young man a beautiful suit and asked him to drive with him. Of course the cat went, too, and as they passed along he waved his paw and said, 'All these lands belong to my master.' By and by they came to a castle where lived a giant. So the cat ran ahead, and said to the giant, who was sitting in his big room; 'I hear you can change yourself into anything. Let me see if you can turn into a mouse!' 'That's easy!' laughed the foolish giant. Whereupon this wise cat ate him up. And when the king arrived, he said, 'Here is my master's castle;' which so pleased the king that he gave his daughter to wed and the young man never forgot how his cat helped him to fame and fortune. And this cat is my father," concluded little Puss, Junior, with a bow.

ARKVILLE

THE next morning when Puss, Junior, went down to the river, he found his boat was gone.

Walking in the rain

"Now I must trust again to my red-topped boots," he sighed, and at once set off to find his dear father. By and by he saw a little man in the distance, who, on coming nearer, turned out to be Tom Thumb.

Puss picked him up and placing him on his shoulder, set off once more. But, goodness me! It soon began to rain, and Tom Thumb crept into a pocket to keep dry.

Towards the middle of the day they arrived on the outskirts of a small village. In the distance they could hear the strokes of a hammer, and then, now and again, the whirr of a saw cutting into hard wood.

"What's going on, I wonder?" said Tom Thumb; "sounds as if they were building a house."

"Don't know," answered Puss, "but let's hurry, for I am soaked to the skin."

On arriving in the village they saw what appeared to be an immense boat in the early stages of construction. It was being erected in the city square, the little park that stood in the midst of the stores and houses.

Drawing nearer they heard a voice singing:

"Noah of old did build an Ark
Of spicy gopherwood and bark
To float upon the deluge dark.
Now on this Ark they had no sail,
For it was made (and true the tale)
Without a mast to break the gale."

When Puss and Tom halted at the side of the Ark a kind-looking man stopped his hammering and said:

"It's going to rain for forty days and forty nights. There's going to be an awful deluge. You'd better stay in Arkville and get aboard the Ark as soon as it's finished. If you don't you'll get drowned."

"He speaks the truth, I'm thinking," answered Tom Thumb, peeping out of Puss, Junior's, pocket. "It looks to me as if the rain were never going to stop."

"My good sir," said Puss, turning to the man, "it seems to me your advice is good. We'll stay in Arkville for a few days. But where shall we stop? Is there a hotel near?"

"Over yonder is the Hotel Ark," said the man. "I'm the proprietor, and my name is Noah. Go in and make yourselves at home. My sons and I will follow you shortly. We have a few more nails to drive before we quit for the day."

HOTEL ARK

THE Hotel Ark was a comfortable sort of a place, not very up-to-date, but with enough conveniences to make the traveler perfectly at home. He felt even more so after meeting the proprietor's wife, Mrs. Noah, a motherly-looking woman, with kind blue eyes and red cheeks.

"Come right in," she said as Puss, Junior, and Tom Thumb, both wet to the skin, rapped on the door.

"You'd best dry yourselves in the kitchen," she said, leading them down a narrow hall. "It's so warm in there you'll be dry in no time."

This was good news to our two small travelers, for their teeth were chattering like twenty-four small white horses on a red hill.

"Here's a chair for you and here's a chair for Tom Thumb," said Mrs. Noah. "I'm not sure about your name, but I can't mistake that of your little friend." Puss, Junior, turned and bowed. Although he was wet, he did not forget his manners. "My name is Puss in Boots, Junior."

"To be sure, to be sure," cried Mrs. Noah, "I might have known it."

The kitchen fire was burning merrily, bright flames shot

up the chimney and sparks from the wood flew out like stars upon the polished floor. Puss pulled off his dripping hat and laid it down on the chair. The feather was much bedraggled and had lost its wave. Tom Thumb undid his coat and hung it up, and then took off his shoes and placed them close to the hearth.

"I think my boots are half full of water," said Puss, Junior; "they are as heavy as lead, and when I walk they make a funny noise." They certainly were full of water, for when Puss finally got them off and turned them over, a stream of water ran down the floor, nearly washing Tom Thumb across the room.

By the time their clothes were dry, Noah and his three sons arrived for supper.

"Still raining!" said the good man, as he closed the door. "I must finish the Ark to-morrow. We may find a lake around the hotel by the morning. Who can tell? But I shall be ready to take in all the animals and my family by noon at the latest."

ALL ABOARD

IT was still raining when Puss, Junior, and Tom Thumb awoke. They had spent a comfortable night at the Hotel Ark and felt much refreshed. After a hearty breakfast they again looked out of the window. The rain was still coming down in torrents, and water lay inches deep upon the street. The Hotel Ark was surrounded by a shallow lake which, however, was growing deeper every minute.

Puss, Junior, stepped out upon the veranda and looked over the village square. Through the rain he could make out the outlines of the Ark. Just then a voice began to sing:

"He built it high, he built it strong,

He built it wide, he built it long,

To hold a jolly, motley throng."

Pretty soon Noah himself came splashing through the water toward the hotel.

"There is no time to lose," he cried, "the Ark will soon be afloat. Mother, make haste. Tell the girls to come along. We've no time to lose." Mrs. Noah appeared almost immediately, followed by the wives of her three sons. Lifting up their skirts, they waded after Noah. Puss, Junior, picked up Tom Thumb and placed him on his shoulder. From far and near, from the forest and the plain, from everywhere, the animals came hurrying up.

"There were the Elephant and Bee,

The Hippopotamus and Flea,

The tall Giraffe and Chick-a-dee,

The Cock-a-doodle and the Ass,

And three young men, each with his lass,

Shem, Ham and Japhet had a pass!

Noah of old, and Noah's dame,

I think I never heard her name,

But she went in tho' all the same."

"This reminds me of the circus," laughed Puss, Junior. "I once was with a circus; three days or so; whenever I see an elephant I think of my circus days."

Animals coming to the ark

"Let down the gang-plank," commanded Noah, and soon a long procession of animals began to enter the Ark. The rain kept up its heavy downpour and by noon the water was waist deep. All the smaller animals had come aboard and Captain Noah (as he was now called) felt certain by evening he would be able to start on his voyage.

PRECIOUS MOTHER GOOSE

AS the last animal came on deck and the Noah boys hauled in the gang-plank, the ark began rolling heavily, for the wind was high and the water rough. "Are we sure every one is aboard?" asked Captain Noah,

"But best of all, my little dears,

'Twill most delight your listening ears,

So give with me three mighty cheers,

To hear that sheltered by that truce,

Loved more than Monkey, Owl or Moose,

In walked Your Precious Mother Goose!"

If there was anyone more delighted than Puss, Junior, he could not be found aboard the Ark. To once more see Mother Goose who had so kindly carried him on her Gander many miles filled him with delight. He ran forward to greet her as she alighted from her faithful Gander.

"Mother Goose! Mother Goose!" cried Puss, "I'm so glad to see you again."

"Let us go in. It's getting dreadfully wet outside," she replied giving him a big hug.

Inside the cabin all was dry and cheerful. Mrs. Noah had

the stove burning brightly and her three daughter-in-laws were busy; getting supper.

"Let me take your bonnet," said Mrs. Noah and before that dear old lady could remove her headgear, Mrs. Noah had taken out the big pin and undone the strings.

"There, make yourself comfortable," she cried, pushing forward a rocking-chair. "And have you found your father?" asked the Gander, for he and Puss were having a fine time talking over old times.

"No, not yet," answered Puss sadly, "But I hear he is Seneschal at the castle of my Lord of Carabas."

"You must be patient," answered the Gander. "And go in search of more adventures."

"Yes," answered Puss, "and I have with me my good comrade, Tom Thumb."

"All ashore that's going ashore," shouted the hoarse voice of Captain Noah. Then came the tinkle-jingle of the bell and the Ark quivered from bow to stern, and in another moment was off on the dark waters.

CAPTAIN NOAH

THE first night on the Ark was most uncomfortable. It was not an easy thing to provide sleeping quarters for the animals, and although Captain Noah and his three sons did their best, from the complaints that were heard in the morning, it was easy to see that very few were satisfied.

"We must get up a set of rules and regulations," said Captain Noah at the breakfast table. "It's all very well to carry a cargo of coal or salt but when it comes to animals it's quite another thing. Each animal is so blamed different," and Captain Noah heaved a great sigh as he lifted the steaming cup of coffee to his lips.

Puss, Junior, and Tom Thumb had risen with the sun—that is, I should say, at an early hour, for of course there was no sun. No, indeed, there was nothing but rain and a wide expanse of water. Water, water, everywhere, but not a speck of dirt. The whole world seemed nothing but water. The only thing that wasn't water was the Ark and its passengers.

However, this did not keep Puss, Junior, and Tom Thumb from eating a hearty breakfast. They were good travelers, whether by land or sea, and to Puss, who had passed through many a dangerous adventure, the present situation seemed one of great interest.

Mother Goose was also in high spirits. Turning to Captain Noah, she said:

"My dear Captain, if it weren't for you, I hardly know what in the world I should have done. To fly on gander-back through the rain for forty days and nights would be impossible, so I have you to thank for my deliverance."

"Don't mention it, my dear Mother Goose," replied Captain Noah. "I did only what was my duty. You know, I have always been the Weatherman of Arkville, and, if I do say it, I have hit the mark every time. I knew, in fact, I felt, that we were to have forty days and forty nights of rain. For the last two weeks I have published this in the Arkville News. To have the Ark finished in time was my greatest ambition, and now to reach Mount Ararat will be the crowning joy of my career.

"We didn't know where we were at,

One wide river,

Until we bumped on Ararat,

One wide river to cross."

"I've so often heard that song at the Minstrels," said Mother Goose, "that I believe it's really coming true."

FORTY DAYS AND FORTY NIGHTS

THE Ark was an exceedingly good sea craft. It rode the waves and breasted the gale without a mishap. Some of the animals became sea sick. But this, of course, was to be expected. Even Captain Noah himself felt rather queer at times, and as for little Tom Thumb, he kept to his bed for almost a week. Puss, Junior, proved to be a very fine sailor. Not once did he feel the least bit ill, and was able to help Mrs. Noah attend to the sick passengers.

Of all the animals, however, the elephant was the most sea sick.

"Of course, it had to be the biggest animal!" said Captain Noah at breakfast one morning. "Too bad, my dear," turning to Mrs. Noah, "that you have such an unwieldy patient on your hands." Mrs. Noah only smiled.

"He does very little complaining," replied Mrs. Noah, "that is one thing to be thankful for. Now, take the little black ant. She does nothing but complain all the time. I'd rather attend to the elephant ten times over."

"Well, mother, you always had something to be thankful for at the Ark Hotel. I'm glad that on board the Ark you still keep your cheerful disposition!" answered Captain Noah.

But, oh, dear me! Pretty soon Puss, Junior, and Tom Thumb wondered if the forty days and forty nights would ever end and if the rain would ever stop. At last, one day, it seemed as if the sun were trying to break through the clouds. And then, all of a sudden, the rain ceased, and in the distance the dim outline of a mountain appeared through the mist.

At once the animals began to sing:

"We didn't know where we were at,

One wide river,

Until we bumped on Ararat,

One wide river to cross."

As if in obedience to the words of the song the Ark grounded, the sun came out from the clouds, and every one knew the voyage was at an end, for

"The Ark she landed high and dry,

One wide river,

And the monkey kissed the cow good-by,

One wide river to cross."

In a few minutes the gang-plank was lowered and the animals landed. Captain Noah was the last to leave.

"Well," he exclaimed, "we have passed through an awful lot. But we're safe on land again." "Hurrah!" shouted all the animals, "we're safe at last!"

UP AND DOWN

WHAT is the news of the day,
Good neighbors, I pray?
They say the balloon
Is gone up to the moon.

It was the day of the county fair. Puss, Junior, had bought his ticket and stood looking about him uncertain what to do.

"They say the balloon has gone up to the moon," cried the crowd.

"Why, I've been up to the moon," said Puss, Junior, "but never will I get excited over that?" But, nevertheless, he walked up to the balloon man and asked. "When does your next balloon go up?"

"In about five minutes," replied the owner of the air craft. "We have an ascension every half hour."

"Well," replied our little hero, "I would like to be one of your passengers!"

"Pay your shilling and you shall have a seat in the basket," answered the owner.

Puss leaned over the edge

After waiting for perhaps an hour the basket car was

filled. My, how the people cheered as the balloon ascended, and when it had almost reached the clouds Puss leaned over the edge of the basket and threw little notes down to the people below. "Tell my good friends that Puss in Boots, Junior, has gone up in a balloon," he wrote on one of them.

On another, he scribbled, "Puss in Boots, Junior, is about to visit the Man in the Moon."

"You had better be careful," said the owner of the balloon, "how do I know we'll reach the moon?"

"If you follow my directions you will," replied Puss, Junior, "for I have been there before and, to tell you the truth, it is a most remarkable place. The moon is an unexplored country."

"Well, I'll take your word for it," said the navigator of the balloon express. "I don't know much about these sky roads, but if you'll kindly consent to tell me where to steer my air craft, perhaps we'll reach the moon without a mishap."

"Trust to me," said Puss, Junior, "for I have traveled far and if I don't know the way to the moon, my name is not Puss in Boots, Junior."

So the owner of the balloon steered the big air craft straight up to the sky. Oh, dear me! But strange things will happen! For as they were sailing along as smoothly as could be, there came a sudden gust of wind, and the balloon, instead of pointing for the big, round moon that shone like a silver dollar overhead, suddenly swerved to one side and before anyone could say "Jack Robinson" there was a dreadful explosion and Puss and his fellow passengers found themselves falling to the earth.

"Good gracious!" exclaimed Puss. "What's the matter?"

Before his question was answered the balloon crashed into a big willow tree.

ROCK-A-BY

IT was lucky that the balloon fell into the big willow tree, as I mentioned in the last story, for otherwise Puss, Junior, and his fellow passengers might have been badly hurt. As it happened, they were none the worse except for a few scratches. Puss pulled himself together and after arranging his clothes, which were torn and mussed by the branches of the tree, looked about him. Suddenly, he heard the cry of a baby, and turning around, he saw a little cradle swinging back and forth. It was fastened securely to a limb, and rocked to and fro as the breeze blew through the trembling leaves.

"Rock-a-by, baby, upon the tree top!

When the wind blows the cradle will rock;

When the bough breaks the cradle will fall;

Down tumbles baby, cradle and all."

"S-s-sh!" cried the balloon man, "We will wake the baby if we are not careful."

"Won't it be sad if the bough breaks," said Puss, Junior, "it will be almost as bad for the baby as it was for us when the balloon fell into this tree."

"It might be worse," said one of the passengers, who stood near them on a limb, looking anxiously to the ground.

"Suppose we take down the cradle," said the balloon man.

"Somebody must have hung it up here," said Puss, "we have no right to take it down; it's not our baby."

"You are perfectly right," said another passenger. "It isn't our cradle and it isn't our baby, so the best thing for us to do is to leave the cradle and climb down."

As soon as the passengers were once more upon the ground they demanded their fare back, saying that they had paid for a trip to the moon, and not for a fall into a willow tree.

"This doesn't seem quite fair to me," remarked the balloon man, looking ruefully at his wrecked balloon. "I don't think I should give you back more than half, for the first part of the journey was successful."

"You didn't keep to your bargain," cried Puss, stoutly; "and besides, you endangered our lives. I don't want to pay to go up in the air a little way and then be hurled down into a willow tree; it takes all the niceness out of the way up and makes the way down too dangerous."

So the balloon man paid back the money and turned away. "Why don't you take the basket car with you?" asked Puss, Junior.

"It's too big to carry," replied the balloon man. "I'll come around for it to-morrow with a horse and wagon."

Pretty soon all the passengers had gone, leaving Puss alone under the willow tree. All of a sudden the baby began to cry, so Puss sang softly:

"Hush-a-by, baby, upon the tree top,

When the wind blows the cradle will rock."

And then the baby stopped crying, so Puss turned away and entered the old mill that stood in the shade of the old willow tree.

THE ROCK-A-BY BABY

"WELCOME, Sir Cat," said the dusty miller. "Sit down and tell me the news." But just then a sweet voice commenced to sing:

Down in the village all the long day
Mother's been toiling the hours away;
While up in the tree-top beneath the blue sky
Baby has rocked to the wind's lullaby.
Waiting is over, my sweet little one,
Mother is here for her own blue-eyed son.
Home we will go, and baby shall rest,
All the night through on mother's warm breast.

"Dearie me," suddenly exclaimed the dusty miller, "how tired she looks," and he walked to the door.

"Let me carry the cradle," said Puss, and lifting it on his shoulder, followed the grateful little woman down the road.

When they reached the house Puss was tired, for the cradle was heavy, and had nearly slipped off his shoulder two or three times, and once, when the baby caught hold of it, Puss nearly stumbled.

"Come and rest," said the baby's mother, opening the little wicket gate in the white fence. Puss looked up at the pretty porch, covered with a honeysuckle vine. "Thank you," he answered, "I will," and he set the cradle down on the floor.

"Please look after the baby," said the little mother, "while I get the supper?"

"I'll try," said Puss, "but I'm not used to babies, and perhaps he'll roll off the porch."

"Oh, you can keep him from doing that," replied the little mother, "he's the best baby in the world!" So Puss sat down and played with him for almost half an hour. By and by a little bird began to sing:

"Dance to your daddie,

My bonnie laddie;

Dance to your daddie, my bonnie lamb.

You shall get a fishy

On a little dishy;

You shall get a fishy when the boat comes home."

Pretty soon after that the little mother carried the baby into the house.

Puss followed her into a cozy room, where, on the mantlepiece, stood a tick-tocky clock, just striking six. The tablecloth was spread and everything was ready for supper. Over in the corner hung a cage, in which sat a big green parrot.

"Polly want a cracker?" asked Puss.

"No, I don't want a cracker," replied the parrot; "I want a little mouse."

"What!" cried Puss, "you don't mean to say you don't like crackers?"

"I'm tired of them," said the parrot.

"Did you ever eat a raisin cracker?" said Puss, with a grin.

But the parrot didn't reply. Pretty soon he opened the door of his cage and came out. Puss was all alone in the room, for the mother had taken the baby upstairs.

"I'm going to fly out of the window," exclaimed the parrot. "I'm tired being alone all day in this house." And before Puss could stop him, he opened the window and flew away.

"The parrot's gone!" cried Puss running to the foot of the stairs. Then he rushed out into the yard and found the parrot perched on the limb of an old apple tree.

"I won't come back!" he cried. "I won't!"

SAILORS TWO

"THERE was an old woman of Glo'ster,
Whose parrot two guineas it cost her,
But his tongue never ceasing,
Was vastly displeasing
To the talkative woman of Glo'ster."

Now as soon as the old woman who lived next door saw Puss, Junior, climb the tree to catch the parrot who had flown out of the window, she cried, "Don't let the pussy cat get you, Polly."

But goodness me! As soon as the old woman's parrot heard that he was up in the tree with the other parrot, and then they both began to scream, "I won't come back! I won't come back!"

"I don't care what they do," said the old woman, "I'd much rather have a cat for a pet than a parrot, anyway. He has been a dreadful care ever since my son, who is a sailor, brought him home."

So Puss looked down from the tree and said, "Then would you rather I didn't catch your parrot?"

"Yes, let him go," said the old woman.

"But I must catch the other one," said Puss.

"Well, you'll have to get a pair of wings, my dear Sir Cat," cried the parrot. "You may be Puss in Boots, Junior, but you can't fly. So I bid you farewell," and away he flew, and then the old woman's parrot clapped his wings and followed him.

So there was nothing for Puss to do but come down from the tree. And then all of a sudden the old woman cried, "Why, here comes my son," and a sailor boy jumped over the fence and threw his arms around her.

"My ship just got in to-day, mother," he cried, giving her a big hug. And after that he looked at Puss, and said, "Shiver my timbers, but that's a fine cat you have, mother."

"He's not mine," answered the old woman, "but I wish he would stay with us, my parrot has just flown away."

"Thank you, madam," said Puss, "but I must be on my way to find my father, Puss in Boots."

"We sail to-morrow," said the sailor boy, "why don't you come aboard ship? You'll have a fine trip, and maybe you'll find your father at the first sea-port we reach."

"Good idea," cried Puss, "I'll go with you."

"All right, my hearty," cried the sailor boy, slapping Puss on the back, "you and I will be pals. A sailor's life is the life for me."

"Then I'll be a sailor, too," cried Puss, "and to-morrow we will sail the ocean blue."

A WONDERFUL SHIP

"I SAW a ship a-sailing,
A-sailing on the sea;
And it was full of pretty things
For baby and for me."

"Hurrah!" cried Puss, Junior, "A sailor's life is the life for me." The good ship was at the dock, and her crew of sailor boys were ready to cast off the mooring lines. Puss, Junior, had been promised a sailor-suit as soon as the ship's tailor had the time to make it.

Just then the little woman who hung her baby's cradle on the willow tree by the old mill, came walking down to the dock.

"Are you going, too?" asked Puss, helping her with the cradle, for she had walked a long way and was very tired.

"Yes, indeed," she replied, "because it's full of pretty things for baby and for me."

"How jolly!" cried Puss, dancing about on his toes. "We'll have a fine trip."

"That's what the 'rusty, dusty' miller said," cried the baby's mother. "He told me this morning when I put the cradle in the 'Rock-a-by' willow tree that the ship was sailing to-day and that they needed a cook; so I'm going to ask the Captain if I may cook and bake for you all. I know how to make the nicest cookies you ever ate. You just wait and see what nice things we will have to eat."

Then Puss helped her over the gang-plank, for the crew was busy loading the good ship with all kinds of things.

Pretty soon the miller came running down the dock. "Here is a sack of flour," he panted, "I thought you might need some for muffins."

"Isn't that fine?" said Puss, leaning over the rail. "There's nothing like having plenty of food aboard in case the voyage is a long one."

"I don't know where we are bound," said the baby's mother, "but baby will like it, I'm sure. One can 'rock-a-by baby' on the sea as well as on the old willow tree."

"I heard," said the 'rusty, dusty' miller, as he laid the heavy sack of flour on the deck, and wiped the perspiration from his forehead, "that

"There were sweetmeats in the cabin,

And apples in the hold;

The sails were made of silk,

And the masts were made of gold."

"Why, so they are," cried Puss, gazing up at the beautiful tall shining masts. "They are of gold, of course they are. Look, baby," he cried, "see the gold masts."

"He's too young to know whether they are made of gold or good old oak," said his mother, "but we'll teach him to be a good sailor, won't we, Puss, dear?"

ALL ABOARD!

"ALL aboard!" shouted the Captain.

"The four and twenty sailors
That stood between the decks,
Were four and twenty white mice,
With chains about their necks."

"There's a locket fastened to every chain," cried Puss. "What pretty lockets."

"Each little sailor mouse has a picture of his mother in his locket," said the Captain, who stood near by giving the orders. Now,

"The captain was a duck,
With a packet on his back;
And when the ship began to move
The Captain cried, 'Quack! Quack!'"

"Hello!" said Puss, Junior, stretching out his right paw. "Hello, Captain! Aren't you the duck that took me across the pond on your back a long, long time ago. You told me about your cousin, the Golden Goose, don't you remember?"

"So I did," said the Captain, looking Puss over. "Shiver my timbers if you're not Puss, Junior!"

"The very same," replied Puss.

"And haven't you found your daddy yet?" asked the Captain as his good ship swung away from the dock, her silk sails filling with the breeze until they looked like great big balloons cut in half.

"No, Captain," replied Puss, sadly, "I haven't."

"Well, we'll ask for him at every port," replied the kind master of the good ship, which was now rolling and dipping in the most graceful way possible. "I'll ask every old land lubber on the docks when we touch port. We'll hear some news, never fear." And then the Captain went over to tell the man at the tiller where to go. The "man" at the wheel was a little white mouse, but he knew how to steer the ship as well as any pilot, let me tell you.

"I don't have to rock the cradle," said the baby's mother, with a smile, looking up at Puss, as he tip-toed over to where she sat.

"No, he's fast asleep," replied Puss, "and the big blue ocean is rocking him better than the willow tree."

"Rock-a-by baby, safe on the ship,
Where the foam-crested billows ripple and dip;
And the breeze from the land of the big yellow moon
Is turning the sail to a great white balloon."

"Where did you hear that pretty song?" asked Puss.

"Why, I just made it up," replied the baby's mother.

"Mothers always do that when they rock their little ones to sleep, you know."

OLD TOM

THE next morning the good ship came in sight of an old seaport. The harbor was very safe, for a tall white lighthouse stood upon the rocks to guide the sailors, and bellbuoys clanged their solemn warning from the dangerous reefs. In the distance rose a church spire, and near it stood a little red schoolhouse with a flag flying in the breeze. Down on the wharf ran a low row of buildings, worn and battered, where the old sailors lounged and told stories of their early days.

Pretty soon the good ship came about, and with her silken sails flapping in the wind, drifted up to the dock.

"Make fast!" shouted the Captain. The four and twenty little sailor mice jumped nimbly on the dock, and in a few minutes made the silk ropes fast to the posts. Then the good ship came to a standstill, and the gang-plank was lowered.

"All ashore that's going ashore!" quacked the captain.

"Oh Captain Duck," cried Puss, Junior, "we don't have to land, do we?"

"No," replied the Duck. "But you may go ashore for a little while if you wish. We don't sail for two hours."

"All right!" replied Puss, "I'll take a run on the grass," and he walked down the gang-plank across the old wharf, until he came to a path, well worn by the sailors who for years had carried the cargoes up to the little village. Under a tree close by sat an old sailor. He was smoking a big black pipe as contentedly as could be. But as soon as he saw Puss he took it out of his mouth.

"Ahoy, my breezy little reefer," he cried.

"Good morning," replied Puss.

"Don't be in a hurry," said the old sailor. "Just moor your little hulk alongside of old Tom."

"What's the matter, my breezy little skipper?" asked the old sailor after a few minutes silence, for, Puss, you see, didn't know what to say.

"Nothing," replied Puss, sadly, "only, I can't find my father, the famous Puss in Boots."

"What did he look like?" asked the old sailor, with a grin.

"He looked like me——or, rather, I look like him," replied Puss.

"Well, my merry little sandpiper!" cried the old salt, "you should have stayed at home!"

"I don't agree with you," said Puss stoutly, "I wanted to see the world."

"Give me your flipper," said the old sailor kindly. "Good luck to ye. I hope you find your daddy."

A NEW PASSENGER

PUSS, JUNIOR, waved his paw to the old sailor, who put his pipe back in his mouth and smoked away contentedly under the shady tree. All of a sudden a pretty little girl jumped out from behind a stone wall.

"Bobby Shafto's gone to sea,
Silver buckles on his knee;
He'll come back and marry me,
Pretty Bobby Shafto.
Bobby Shafto's fat and fair,
Combing down his yellow hair;
He's my love for aye and ere,
Pretty Bobby Shafto."

"Hello," said Puss when she had finished her song.

"Did you just get off that pretty ship," she asked.

"Yes, Miss," replied Puss.

"Was Bobby Shafto on board?"

"I didn't see him," replied Puss. "Did you expect him?"

"I don't know," replied the little girl, "but I run down to look every time a ship comes to the old dock. And I always ask the old sailor who sits on the bench over there if he has seen my Bobby."

"You're looking for your Bobby, and I'm searching for my daddy," said Puss, sadly. And then he told the little girl how discouraged he was because in all his travels he had not yet found him.

And then, all of a sudden, they heard a voice calling, "All aboard!"

"Goodness!" exclaimed Puss, "I must hurry; the ship's going to sail. Good-by!" and off he ran to the dock as fast as he could.

"Wait for me," called out the little girl, "I guess I'll go, too. I may find Bobby Shafto."

"Hurry, hurry!" cried Puss, looking back. "I'll run ahead and ask the Captain to wait."

And it was lucky he did, for the gang-plank was being hauled in just as he arrived. "Wait for us!" he shouted.

"Why, I don't see anybody else," said the Captain, as Puss stepped aboard.

"Yes, there is," answered Puss, "There she comes!"

And in another minute, with her bonnet strings streaming in the wind, the little girl came running down the dock.

"Thank you for waiting," she cried, turning to the Captain. "I'd have been so disappointed if you had left me behind."

And then she stood close to Puss as the good ship left the dock. "Good luck, my little skipper," shouted the old sailor.

"Good-by," cried Puss, waving his cap to the old salt.

OVER THE WATER

WHEN the old dock and the gray-haired sailor, the tall church spire and the flag on the little red schoolhouse were out of sight, Puss, Junior, turned to the little girl and said: "Let's go down in the cabin. I'll show you the cutest little baby you ever saw. It's the 'rock-a-by, baby, upon-the-tree-top.' His mother always hung the cradle on a willow tree so that the breeze might rock him to sleep. But now the ocean does the rocking and baby sleeps almost all the time."

So the little girl followed Puss down the stairs to the cabin, where they heard a sweet voice singing:

"Over the water, and over the sea,
And over the water to Charley.
I'll have none of your horrid beef,
Nor I'll have none of your barley:
But I'll have some of your very best flour
To make a white cake for my Charley."

"S-s-sh!" said the mother of the baby as Puss and the little girl came in.

"Are you going to make a cake with the flour the miller

brought on board?" asked Puss in a whisper.

"Yes," said the baby's mother. "But what's your name?" turning to the little girl.

"She's looking for Bobby Shafto," answered Puss.

"What's your name, little girl," asked the rock-a-by-baby's mother.

"Alice," said the little girl.

"A pretty name."

"I'm glad you like it," said the little girl. "And what is yours?"

"Mine? Oh, you can call me 'The Rock-a-by Baby's Mother.'"

"Let's go out on deck," suggested Puss. "Won't you come, too?" he asked, turning to the baby's mother.

Rolling in the sea were huge black porpoises. Over and over they rolled like great footballs. Flying fish rose out of the water, and overhead the gulls sailed back and forth on their great wings. The breeze was blowing strong and steady, and now and then the salt spray came over the railing. Some of it wet Puss, Junior's, whiskers.

"Did you get wet?" asked Alice.

"Not much," said Puss. "Besides, I don't care for a little spray, anyway."

"Come over here and sit down on this coil of rope," said the Rock-a-By-Baby's Mother, and I'll sing you a song:

"Rock-a-by, rock-a-by on the deep blue,

Sailor Boy, Mother is dreaming of you.

Thinking of Sailor Boy out on the foam,

Hoping that Sailor Boy soon will be home."

CUSTARD AND MUSTARD

FOR several days the good ship, with the four and twenty sailor mice and the duck captain, sailed over the big blue sea. Puss, Junior, learned to climb the mast and to run out to the very tip of the great boom to tie a rope for Captain Duck when it was blowing a gale. The Rock-a-By-Baby's Mother made a most delicious cake with the flour which the 'rusty, dusty' miller had sent on board, and altogether it was a most enjoyable trip, and when the good ship put into port on the fifth day everybody was sorry.

Even the little girl who was waiting for Bobby Shafto to come home told Puss she had forgotten all about him.

Well, as soon as the ship was fast to the dock, Puss said good-by to Captain Duck and the sailor mice.

"I hope Bobby Shafto will return soon," he whispered to the little girl as he kissed her good-by.

"I shall miss you very much," he said to the Rock-a-By-Baby's mother.

"Will you, my dear Puss?" she answered, giving him a hug. "You're a dear little cat! I hope you soon find your father. When you do, tell him he has a fine little son—tell him that from me, won't you?"

And after that Puss went upon his way, and by and by,

after a while he found himself on a broad highway. "I wonder what will happen next?" he said to himself, and just then he came to a small house near the road. So he stopped at the front gate to listen to a sweet voice singing:

"When Jacky's a very good boy
He shall have cakes and a custard;
But when he does nothing but cry
He shall have nothing but mustard."

Puss opened the gate and peeped through the window. In the centre of the room stood a small boy, wiping his eyes with a little pink handkerchief.

"Nothing but mustard," repeated his mother, "if you don't stop crying."

"Meow!" cried Puss at the window. "Won't you give me some custard?" And then, my goodness! didn't that little boy stop crying!

"Look at the cat with boots on!" he cried, running up to the window.

"You both shall have some custard," said Jack's mother, "and then you may go out to the swing and have a good time."

Well, it didn't take long to eat the custard, and then Jacky and Puss went out under the big tree.

"Swing high, swing low.
Away we go,
Up to the skies,
Down to the ground;
This is the finest
Sport I've found,"

sang Puss, Junior.

"After supper, Jacky, I'll tell you how I was a sailor boy for almost a week on the ocean blue!"

ROWLEY FROG

NOW let me think what happened after Puss finished telling how he had been a sailor for a week on the ocean blue.

Oh yes, of course. He had scarcely said good-by to the little boy when whom should he meet but Mr. Rowley Frog and a big rat.

Frog

"So you're going to make a call on Mrs. Mousey," said Puss, as he and Mr. Rowley Frog and the rat reached the dusty highway.

"Yes, sir-ee," replied Mr. Rowley Frog. "She lives just over there." And when Puss looked across the meadow he saw a cute little house.

"Looks like a pretty nice little place," said the rat; "let's hurry along." So all three started off on a run.

When they came to the door of Mousey's hall,

Heigh-ho, says Rowley.

They gave a loud knock, and they gave a loud call.

Pray, Mrs. Mouse, are you within?

Heigh-ho, says Rowley!

Oh, yes, kind sirs, I'm sitting to spin.

"I guess she's too busy," said Puss. "We'd better not interrupt her."

"Nonsense," replied Mr. Rowley Frog, bowing to Mrs. Mousey, who happened just then to look out of her little window. Then Mr. Rat took off his cap and said:

"Pray, Mrs. Mouse, will you give us some beer?"

Heigh-ho, says Rowley.

"For Froggy and I are fond of good cheer."

"Indeed, I will not," said Mrs. Mousey. "You ought to be ashamed of yourself! And as for Mr. Anthony Rowley, he must throw away that horrid cigar if he wants to call on me."

Well, goodness gracious! Didn't Mr. Rowley look ashamed! He threw his cigar away at once, and Mr. Rat hid behind Puss, he was so embarrassed, and as soon as Mrs. Mousey saw that they were both truly sorry for what they had done, she smiled and said:

"Pray, Mr. Frog, will you give us a song?"
Heigh-ho, says Rowley.
"But let it be something that's not very long."
"Indeed, Mrs. Mouse," replied the Frog,
Heigh-ho, says Rowley.
"I've caught quite a cold, for it's damp in the bog."
"Since you have caught cold, Mr. Frog," Mousey said,
Heigh-ho, says Rowley.
"I'll sing you a song that I have just made."

But first she opened the door and invited them in. "I'm not afraid of you," she said to Puss, "for I know you are Mr. Puss in Boots, Junior."

Well, just as soon as they were all seated, she began to sing:

"Mrs. Mousey has a housey,
Very small and trim,
Nice Swiss cheeses good for sneezes,
Filled up to the brim.
Also candy, fine and dandy,
Ice cream soda, too,
If you're nice to little mice,
I'll give some to you."

"I'll see that my two small friends behave," said Puss, with a grin.

MRS. MOUSEY

"WHAT will you have?" Mrs. Mousey asked Puss, Junior, as she opened the cupboard door.

"I'll have a strawberry ice-cream soda," said Puss. So Mrs. Mousey poured some red syrup into the glass and dropped in a ball of ice cream, and after that she held the glass under a regular soda-fountain spigot which was fastened to a cute little ice-box. "Fiz-z-z, fiz-z-z!" went the water until the pink-colored foam almost ran over the edge of the glass. But it didn't. Wasn't that lucky?

"I'll take a pink and white peppermint stick," said Mr. Rowley Frog, and Mr. Rat said, "Cheese, if you please!" when Mrs. Mousey asked him what he would have.

"But while they were all a merry-making,

Heigh-ho!" says Rowley.

"A cat and her kittens came tumbling in."

And, oh dear me! Puss dropped his soda-water glass, and it broke all to smithereens. And then,

The cat she seized the rat by the crown:

Heigh-ho! says Rowley.

The kittens they pulled the little mouse down.

And after that the cat jumped through the open window with the rat and disappeared around the house, and the kittens ran out of the door with poor Mrs. Mouse.

Having sodas

Puss jumped through the window, but before he could catch them they ran into a hole just big enough for them to squeeze through, and Puss was left outside, wondering what to do. The old cat was nowhere to be seen. She had taken good care to get out of sight, for she knew that Puss, Junior, would take Mr. Rat away from her if he ever caught her.

"This put Mr. Frog in a terrible fright,

Heigh-ho, says Rowley!

He took up his hat, and he wished them good night."

"I'll go home to mother," he said when he reached the roadway. "I am getting homesick. I think the old pond is the best place for me."

"Home, sweet home, in the dear old pond,

That is the place for me.

I'll never go even a foot beyond,

I'll sit there and croak, and never will smoke,

In my pond by the grassy lea!"

"That's right," said Puss, as he hurried along with Rowley, who, now that he had made up his mind, could not get home fast enough.

"A wise frog stays in his bog,

And sits and croaks upon his log."

A SAD ENDING

"I'M very sorry for poor little Mrs. Mousey," said Puss, as he and Mr. Rowley Frog hastened toward the pond.

"So am I," answered Rowley. "She was very generous with all her good things to eat."

"And the poor rat," continued Puss. "It was a sad ending to our little feast. I guess he's been eaten up by this time. That naughty old cat looked very hungry."

"Oh dear, oh dear," sobbed Rowley, the tears rolling down his face, "I want to get home. I'll never run away again."

"But as Froggy was crossing over a brook,

Heigh-ho, says Rowley.

A lily-white duck came and gobbled him up,

So there was an end of one, two and three,

Heigh-ho, says Rowley.

The Rat, the Mouse and the little Frog-gee,

With a rowley, powley, gammon and spinach,

Heigh-ho, says Anthony Rowley!"

"This is dreadful," cried Puss, as he saw his small friend disappear down the duck's long neck; "it has been a sad day. All three of my little friends are gone."

"Never mind," cried the lily-white duck, looking up at Puss standing mournfully by the side of the brook, "Frogs are good to eat, and if they will run away from home, it's their own lookout. They should stay in their ponds and not go wandering about strange places."

Puss did not answer. It seemed pretty hard to meet such a sad fate, and he did not like the lily-white duck at all.

"Come, come," cried the duck, "cheer up, I'll ferry you across the brook if you wish to reach the other side."

"That's kind of you," said Puss, seating himself on her back.

"I'm not such a bad sort of duck," she continued, paddling swiftly toward the opposite bank, "but I must eat, and frogs are mighty good eating, let me tell you."

As she finished speaking she waddled up the bank, and Puss sprang nimbly from her back. "Thank you, Mrs. Duck," he said, "indeed, I'm obliged to you; but I wish you hadn't eaten my friend, the little frog."

Just then nine little yellow ducklings waddled toward them. "These are my children," said Mrs. Duck, very proudly.

"How are you, my little ducklets?" cried Puss.

"Quite well, thank you," they answered. It was a pretty sight to see those yellow balls of down cuddle up to their mother, and Puss began to feel that, after all, she must be a good sort of duck, for her children loved her so much. Perhaps he had judged her too harshly for gobbling up the frog, and when she turned to Puss and said:

"Come home with us, Mr. Puss," he forgave her for what she had done, and followed her downy, yellow brood.

BEAVER DAM

PUSS, JUNIOR, had gone but a short distance when he heard a sad voice say:

"Oh dear, I've lost my brother,

Where will I ever find another?

He never should have left the bog,

Alas, Alas! poor Rowley Frog!"

"Dear me," cried Puss to Mrs. Duck and he looked about him for the owner of the sad croaky voice. Pretty soon he saw a big bullfrog in a brook.

"Come along with me," cried Puss, Junior.

Just then a little muskrat jumped out of the water and from behind a tree ran a pretty gray squirrel and a striped chipmunk.

"Did you call us?" they asked Puss all at once.

"No, my little friends," he replied, "but come along," and when they reached Beaver Dam, they looked around to see what had become of the old bullfrog. There he was in the water about halfway down the stream, swimming away for all he was worth.

"Ker-chunk, ker-chunk!" he cried, as he came up to them, "Why don't you wait for a fellow? And why didn't you tell me you were going up stream?"

Puss, Junior, felt very sorry to think that he had really forgotten all about the old bullfrog.

"Well, you got here all right, didn't you?" asked the muskrat. "Now," he continued, "I'm going to knock three times on the dam to let Mr. Beaver know that we would like to cross."

After giving three loud knocks, Mr. Beaver looked over and said: "What's the matter? Who are you? What do you want? Where did you come from? Where are you going?"

"We'll answer the last question first," said Puss, Junior, with a grin. "We'd like to cross over on your beautiful great big dam."

"The toll is a penny," said the beaver, looking them over carefully.

"I haven't got a penny with me," said the little squirrel, "but I have a dandy big nut, if that will do."

"All right," said the beaver, "give me the nut." He put it in his pocket, remarking as he did so, "it looks like a good nut. I only hope I shall not be disappointed when I crack it."

Turning to the chipmunk, he said, "What have you got?"

"A little acorn," answered the chipmunk.

"I don't want any more nuts," said the beaver, disgustedly. "I'm not particularly fond of nuts, anyway. I only took this one from the squirrel because I knew he didn't have anything else."

"Here are two pennies, Mr. Beaver—one for Chipmunk and one for me," said Puss, Junior.

"All right, Sir Cat," said the beaver, "walk across, but see that you do not slip, for the water is very deep on the upper side."

Puss carefully wended his way over, followed by the little squirrel and the chipmunk. The old frog swam over, as did the muskrat. When they all reached the other side, Puss went forward, followed by his small comrades, who stretched out behind him like a funny little army.

They hadn't gone very far, when a rabbit jumped out from behind a bush. Puss, Junior, called out, "Don't be frightened. We won't hurt you."

"Baby!" cried the squirrel, "you're bigger than I am, but you're twice as much afraid."

"I'm going to a wedding," said the rabbit. "I've no time to wait!" and away he went.

"Gracious me!" exclaimed the squirrel. "I had forgotten all about Cock Robin's wedding! I must be going."

"And so must I," cried the chipmunk and the beaver, but what the old bullfrog said I will tell you in the next story.

DUCKLINGS

WELL, you will certainly agree with me that the old bullfrog, in the last story, is a wonderful fellow when you hear what he says about Mrs. Duck, and, it is all in poetry, too.

"Old Mother Duck has hatched a brood
Of ducklings, small and callow;
Their little wings are short, their down
Is mottled gray and yellow."

"There is a quiet little stream,
That runs into the moat,
Where tall green sedges spread their leaves
And water lilies float."

"Close by the margin of the brook
The old duck made her nest,
Of straw, and leaves, and withered grass,
And down from her own breast."

"And there she sat for four long weeks,
In rainy days and fine,
Until the ducklings all came out—
Four, five, six, seven, eight, nine."

"So this is your home," said Puss, Junior, as Mrs. Duck stepped into her nest, followed by her brood.

"One peeped out from beneath her wing,
One scrambled on her back;
"That's very rude," said old Mrs. Duck;
"Get off! quack, quack, quack, quack!"

"What do you do when it rains?" asked Puss, Junior.

"What do we do when it rains?" repeated Mrs. Duck,

"why, what do you suppose a duck's feathers are good for? They shed the water as well as a barn roof. Yes, even better, for feathers are water-proof and shingles are not."

"Well, my good Mrs. Duck, of course it's all right for you and your family, but should it rain, what would I do? I couldn't possibly crawl under your wings."

"Not very well," laughed Mrs. Duck.

"But it's not going to rain," cried one little duck, peering out from between her feathers. "I know it's not going to rain, for there isn't a cloud in the sky."

Then all the little ducklings poked their heads out and cried, "It's not going to rain, it's not going to rain!"

"If it should, and there's no telling lately, for the weather has been so unsettled, I could take you up to the barnyard and introduce you to Molly Head," said Mrs. Duck, turning to Puss, Junior. "She has charge of all the poultry and is a very kind woman, very kind indeed."

"If I knew where to buy an umbrella," said Puss, after a pause, "I wouldn't mind a little shower, but you know how a cat hates to get wet."

"Yes, they make as much fuss over a little water as a hen does," laughed good Mrs. Duck.

A LESSON IN WADDLING

PUSS, JUNIOR, was very tired with his journey, so he cuddled up in the long grass close to Mrs. Duck's nest and he was soon fast asleep. Then Mrs. Duck tucked in her yellow ducklings and they were soon dreaming of nice fat worms and little silver fishes. By and by Mrs. Duck closed first one eye and then the other, and pretty soon she was asleep.

The wind played little lullabys in the tall grass and the brook close by murmured over its pebbly bottom. The crickets in the meadow made sleepy little noises, so that it must have been over an hour before anybody woke up.

"'Tis close," said Mrs. Duck, shoving out
The eggshells with her bill,
"Besides, it never suits young ducks
To keep them sitting still."
So, rising from her nest, she said,
"Now, children, look at me:
A well bred duck should waddle so,
From side to side—d'ye see?"

"I'll play duck too," said Puss, jumping to his feet and

imitating Mrs. Duck. The ducklings looked at Puss in wonder.

"He'd make a fine duck," said one little duckling.

"If he had feathers instead of fur," laughed Mrs. Duck.

"If he had yellow stockings like ours," said another duckling, "instead of red-topped boots."

"Stop your quacking," cried Mrs. Duck. "Did you hear what I said about waddling just now?"

"Yes," said the little ones, and then
She went on to explain:
"A well bred duck turns in his toes
As I do—try again."

Puss, Junior, turned in his toes exactly the way they did, which made them laugh; even Mrs. Duck chuckled. "Look out," she cried, "or Puss, Junior, will do it better than you."

"Thank you, ma'am," said Puss with a grin.

"Won't you try to do better?" said Mrs. Duck, turning to her brood with an anxious expression on her kind face.

"Yes," said the Ducklings, waddling on,
"That's better," said their mother;
"But well bred ducks walk in a row,
Straight, one behind the other."

"I wish I had a drum," cried Puss, "I'd beat time. We could make believe we were soldiers." But Mrs. Duck did not answer. "Do your best," she said to her little brood.

"Yes," said the little ducks again,
All waddling in a row.
"Now to the pond," said old Mrs. Duck.
Splash, splash! and in they go.

"I wish I could swim," cried Puss; "it looks like great sport!"

HOW TO BE A DUCK

"LET me swim first," said old Mrs. Duck,
"To this side, now to that;
There, snap at those great brown-winged flies,
They make young ducklings fat."

"See who can swim the fastest," cried Puss. "Why don't you have a race?" The nine little ducklings stopped.

"Line up in a row," cried Puss, "and when I cry 'Go!' swim as fast as you can, and the one who reaches this bank first wins. I'll give a bright penny to the winner."

All the ducklings arranged themselves in a row, and when Puss cried "One, two, three, go!" they paddled away as hard as they could. Back and forth went their little yellow feet. Such a splashing! Nearer and nearer they came. One little duck flapped his wings upon the water and in this way managed to get ahead. He was the first to land.

"Here is your penny," cried Puss.

"What can I do with it, mother?" he asked.

"You can get a stick of candy to-morrow," replied his mother. "Not this afternoon, for it is time now to go home to the farm.

"Now when you reach the poultry yard
The hen-wife, Molly Head,
Will feed you with the other fowls
On bran and mashed-up bread."

Mrs. Duck came out of the water and shook herself well, sending quite a shower of water in little drops all about her. Puss jumped back to avoid a shower bath. The ducklings stood up on their toes and flapped their small wings. Then off they all went, Mrs. Duck in the lead. Puss followed behind, taking care not to step on the yellow toes of the last duckling.

As they neared the barnyard Mrs. Duck turned and said:

"The hens will peck and fight, but mind,
I hope that all of you
Will gobble up the food as fast
As well bred ducks should do."

The woman who took care of the poultry yard was already there. From a well filled pan she was scattering handfuls of corn in all directions. There were a great many chickens, who darted hither and thither, picking up the grains of corn. When the corn was all gone she set down a dish of food. No sooner had she done this than Mrs. Duck exclaimed:

"You'd better get into the dish
Unless it is too small;
In that case, I should use my foot
And overturn it all."

The ducklings did as they were bid,
And found the plan so good
That from that day the other fowls
Got hardly any food.

"My, but she's a wise old duck," said Puss to himself with a grin.

"WHEN I WAS A LITTLE BOY"

IT was a queer looking house that Puss, Junior, saw in the distance. It seemed more like a box, with another little box tacked on, through the top of which rose a long piece of stove pipe, which, I suppose, served as a chimney, although chimneys are usually made of bricks in Old Mother Goose Country.

On the front porch sat a little old man, smoking a pipe, from which the smoke drifted away in little gray clouds, while the smoke from the stovepipe chimney stretched out like a long black feather.

"Good-day," said Puss, taking off his hat.

"Come and rest beside me," said the old man, pushing forward an armchair. So Puss sat down, and after wiping the perspiration from his forehead remarked, "A warm day, my good sir."

"Yes, indeed," replied the little old man, "but all days seem very much alike to me."

"Do they?" asked Puss. "Why?"

"Well, I'll tell you the story of my life," said the little old man, and, taking his pipe from his lips, he began:

"When I was a little boy
I lived by myself,
And all the bread and cheese I got
I laid upon the shelf.
The rats and the mice
They made such a strife,
That I was forced to go to town,
And buy me a wife.
The streets were so broad,
And the lanes were so narrow,
I was forced to bring my wife home
In a wheelbarrow.
The wheelbarrow broke,
And my wife had a fall.
Farewell wheelbarrow, wife and all."

"And have you lived alone ever since?" asked Puss.

"Yes," replied the old man, "and the mice and the rats give me no peace. They eat up all my cheese and flour."

"I'll help you," said Puss. "Let me stay here to-night, and I'll catch every rat and mouse that bothers you inside the house."

"You can make up poetry as well as I can," said the old man, with a laugh. "Why, that's the first laugh I've had in many a long year. I like you, Sir Cat. You are an obliging sort of person. You shall have the best that my small home affords. I only hope you will rid the place of rats and mice."

"Leave that to me," replied Puss, with a grin.

GOOD RIDDANCE

NOW, let me see. In the last story we left little Puss, Junior, in the house of the old man who brought his wife home in a wheelbarrow. Well, Puss heard him take off his shoes and get into bed, and then out went the light. I guess the old man leaned out of bed and blew it out. But Puss didn't go to bed. Oh, my, no! He slipped off his red-topped boots, so as not to frighten the rats and the mice and stole softly over to the window. The moon was bright and the stars were twinkling in the sky.

"It's a long time since I've been a mouser!" laughed Puss to himself. "I wonder if I have lost my cunning?" And he sat down by the window and crossed his leg over the other. "Not a creature was stirring, not even a mouse," and it was not the night before Christmas, either. Pretty soon the sound of scampering feet caught his ear, and, turning his head, he saw a dozen mice or more running over the floor, and after that two big rats stole softly across the old rag rug in front of the fireplace. With a leap, Puss landed close to the rats, and with his right paw, laid hold of the nearest, and with his left paw caught the other. "Squeak, squeak! Oh, let us go!" they cried.

"Not unless you promise to leave this house," replied

Puss, fiercely, his whiskers standing out straight and his eyes glaring like two balls of fire.

"We will, we will!" squeaked the rats.

"Then go!" cried Puss, "and don't you ever come back!"

"We won't, we won't!" cried the terrified rats.

And after that Puss softly crept into the kitchen, where on the table sat three little mice eating a piece of cake. In a second Puss had them fast in his claws.

"Squeak, squeak!" screamed the little mice.

"I'll spare you," said Puss, glaring at them with eyes as bright as automobile lamps. "I'll let you go if you'll promise to leave this house with all your sisters and brothers and cousins and aunts and fathers and mothers and grandmothers and grandfathers, and all your friends, and everybody else that I can't think of, for I'm so mad I could eat you."

"Oh don't," they cried; "we'll go, we'll go! We'll promise to leave."

And after that the little old man was never bothered with rats and mice.

MISTER FOX

IT was late in the evening as Puss, Junior, entered a gloomy forest. It was very dark beneath the big, tall trees, so by and by he stopped and looked about him, when all of a sudden—

"A fox went out in a hungry plight,

And he begged of the moon to give him light,

For he'd many miles to trot that night."

Well, as soon as the Fox had finished asking Lady Moon to show him the way Puss cried out:

"Oh, Mr. Fox, take me with you, for I'm lost in this forest." But goodness me! the Fox was so frightened at the sound of Puss, Junior's, voice that he jumped behind a tree.

"Who speaks to me?" he asked, faintly.

"Puss in Boots, Junior."

"Ah," replied the Fox, coming out from his hiding place, "now I'm not afraid. At first I thought you were a farmer; farmers don't like me!"

"Why should they?" asked Puss. "You steal their ducks and chickens."

"Softly, softly!" whispered the Fox; "someone may hear you."

"Very well," replied Puss, "I'll whisper if you'll show me the way."

"Come along," replied the Fox. So they walked along through the dark forest, and every now and then the moon peeped through the tree tops to help Mr. Fox find his way, but for all that, the forest was very gloomy and Puss nearly stumbled two or three times and so did Mr. Fox.

"At first he came to a farmer's yard,

Where the ducks and geese declared it hard

That their nerves should be shaken and their rest be marred

By the visit of Mister Fox."

"Do you hear what they say about me?" asked the Fox in a whisper.

"They say you give them bad dreams," replied Puss; "that you keep them awake and ruin their nerves."

"Ha, ha!" laughed Mr. Fox, "what do they expect? Do they imagine I come here to sing them to sleep? To stand under the coop window and sing a lullaby? Ha, ha! I'm very fond of duck and very fond of goose, but not in that way. Oh, my, no!" And he grinned until all his long white teeth shone in the moonlight.

MR. SLIPPER-SLOPPER

WHEN Mr. Fox laughed he showed all his long, sharp teeth, and Puss was mighty glad he had his trusty staff with him in case Mr. Fox became ugly. But nothing unpleasant happened, and by and by they came to the hen-house.

Puss was peeking through a crack in the boards, but before he had time to utter a cry of warning, Mr. Fox,

Seized the black duck by the neck,

And swung her across his back;

The black duck cried out, "Quack! quack! quack!"

With her legs hanging dangling down.

and away he went, out through the door, across the barnyard and up the hill. And I guess Lady Moon wished she hadn't shown that bad old fox the way through the dark forest.

And after that Puss pounded on the kitchen door and shouted, "The fox has run off with the black duck!"

"What's the matter?" asked Mrs. Slipper-Slopper. "Who has taken the black duck?"

"Hurry up!" called Puss. "The fox has a good start; 'twill be hard to catch him."

So Mrs. Slipper-Slopper pulled in her head and pretty soon came thumping down the stairs and opened the door.

"Which way did the fox go?" asked Mr. Slipper-Slopper.

"Up the hill," said Puss.

"Where's my gun?" asked Mr. Slipper-Slopper, turning to his wife.

"Why, don't you remember, John?" she replied. "You lent it to old Neighbor Jones last week."

"So I did," said Mr. Slipper-Slopper. "Too bad!"

"Well, I'm going after him, anyway," cried Mr. Slipper-Slopper, picking up the broom. "If I catch him I'll hit him a whopper!"

"You wouldn't hit an old man like Neighbor Jones?" cried Mrs. Slipper-Slopper excitedly.

"No——the fox," cried Mr. Slipper-Slopper. "I mean the fox."

"You'd better put on your boots," said his wife. "You can't go in your slippers."

A DINNER INVITATION

GOODNESS me, Mr. Slipper-Slopper took so long to pull on his boots that Puss said, "Really, if you don't hurry the fox will be miles away, and you'll never get back your gray goose."

"Yes, John, you had better take this young cat's advice," cried Mrs. Slipper-Slopper.

"Then John, he went up to the hill,

And he blew a blast both loud and shrill;

Says the fox, 'This is very pretty music—still

I'd rather be at my den.'"

"Gracious me!" exclaimed Puss to himself, "Mr. Slipper-Slopper is crazy. Why does he blow his horn? It's bad enough to hunt a fox with a broom!"

"Look here, Mr. Slipper-Slopper," he cried, "you have no boots—you've nothing but slippers. You have no gun—you've nothing but an old broom. And what's more, you have no sense. You deserve to lose your gray goose and your black duck. Good-by." And Puss ran off in disgust.

"I've no use for a man who can't protect his own," he muttered to himself. "I won't help catch that fox. Let him have a feast. He must eat as well as Mr. Slipper-Slopper.

Probably Mr. Slipper-Slopper would have killed the gray goose for dinner in a few days, anyhow."

"Helloa, what are you talking about?" cried Mr. Fox, jumping out from behind a large stone.

"So you think old Slipper-Slopper would have killed the goose and eaten it himself, do you?" asked the fox with a grin.

"Well," answered Puss, startled at the sudden appearance of Mr. Fox, "I thought it pretty mean of you to steal his goose, but now that I've found out what a foolish man Mr. Slipper-Slopper is, I'm glad you have a good dinner in store for yourself and family."

"That's very nice of you," said Mr. Fox, with another grin.

"Neither have I forgotten that you helped me out of the forest," continued Puss, "and I feel very friendly toward you."

"If that's the case," said the fox in a kind voice, "you come home with me and Mrs. Fox will give you some of the best roast duck you ever tasted in your life."

ROAST DUCK

PUSS, JUNIOR, accepted the invitation of Mr. Fox to dine, for he was hungry, and the very thought of roast duck for supper made his mouth water.

"Thank you, Mister Fox," he answered. "Let me carry the duck for you—the goose is enough of a load!"

"You are right," replied the fox, handing the duck to Puss. "It was a hard run up that hill. If I had known the farmer better, however, I wouldn't have hurried so."

"Well, lead the way, and I'll follow," said Puss.

"At last the fox got home to his den;

To his dear little foxes, eight, nine, ten,

Says he, 'you're in luck, here's a good fat duck,

With her legs hanging dangling down.'"

"This is Puss in Boots, Junior," he said, turning to his good wife, Mrs. Fox. "He has carried the duck for me, for I have a big fat goose."

Then Mrs. Fox asked Puss to sit down and rest while she cooked the supper, and the little foxes begged him to tell them a story.

"What kind of a story do you like?" asked Puss.

"Tell them how I crept into the hen-house and got away from old Mr. Slipper-Slopper," said Mr. Fox. "You keep them quiet and I'll pluck off the feathers while Mrs. Fox heats the oven. Then we'll lose no time in roasting the duck."

"All right," replied Puss, "I'll tell them about it," and as soon as Mr. Fox went out of the room Puss commenced.

"Your father and I crept softly into the barnyard and then your daddy tiptoed into the hen-house and said to Madam Goose: 'By your leave, I'll take you away and carry you home to my den Oh!' I'm not quite sure whether he or Madam Goose said 'Oh!' but that doesn't make any difference."

"I think it must have been Madam Goose," said a little fox. "I think she was frightened."

"Maybe you are right," said Puss, with a smile. "At any rate, when your father caught the black duck there was no mistake about what she said, it was 'Quack! quack! quack!'"

Well, just then Mr. Fox came in and said dinner was ready.

"He then sat down with his hungry wife.

They did very well without fork or knife.

They never ate a better goose in all their life;

And the little ones picked the bones!"

And Puss, Junior, had all he could eat, too.

TAFFY

"TAFFY was a Welshman, Taffy was a thief,

Taffy came to my house and stole a piece of beef;

I went to Taffy's house, Taffy wasn't home,

Taffy came to my house and stole a marrow-bone;

I went to Taffy's house, Taffy was in bed,

I took the marrow-bone and beat about his head."

"Well, I guess you did what was right," said Puss, Junior, as he and Tom Thumb neared a butcher shop in a small village.

The butcher, who had just spoken in rhyme, shifted from one foot to the other in an uneasy sort of way. "But that isn't all," he went on to say, in rather an anxious tone of voice.

"Tell us the worst, then," laughed Puss, Junior, who didn't appear very sympathetic, although the name Taffy appealed to him and made him wonder what sort of a person Taffy was.

"The truth of the matter is," the butcher went on to say, "I hit him a bit too hard with the marrow-bone. His head is in bad shape, and the doctor says it will be some weeks yet before Taffy gets out of bed."

"Gracious me!" exclaimed Tom Thumb. "Why weren't you more careful?"

"That's just it," replied the butcher. "Why wasn't I more careful?" And then he gave a sigh and went into his shop to wait on a customer.

"Let's make a call on Taffy," said Puss, Junior. "Somehow, I can't help liking him. I don't know whether it's on account of his name, or not. But Taffy sounds awfully nice to me."

"It tastes awfully good to me," laughed Tom Thumb. "You must have him mixed up with candy. That's the reason you like him, I guess."

"Come on and we'll soon find out," cried Puss, Junior. "I'm curious to see what 'Welsh Taffy' is like." So they both walked up the street, inquiring on the way where Taffy lived. If the house Taffy owned was any indication that Taffy was a nice sort of person, it certainly spoke well for him, for it was the prettiest and most homelike little place Puss had ever seen.

"I like him already," said Puss, as he knocked on the door.

A KIND VISIT

OF course, Taffy didn't come to the door. But a little Welshwoman did, and dropping a courtesy, she invited Puss and Tom Thumb to come in.

"How is Taffy?" Puss asked.

"His head is still painful," replied the little Welshwoman, "but for that he feels quite well, thank you," and she dropped another courtesy.

"May we see him?" asked Tom Thumb.

"Well, that I don't know," she replied, "but I will enquire. Won't you step into the sitting room?" So our two small visitors walked in and sat down. The little canary bird hopped about in her cage and the flowers in the green boxes in the bay-window nodded in the sunlight, as the big old clock in the far corner ticked away the minutes.

"Come up and see Taffy," suddenly cried the voice of the little Welshwoman.

I guess Puss had almost fallen asleep listening to the drowsy tick of the old clock and the low twitter of the canary. Everything was so quiet and home-like it reminded him of his old home when he had prowled about in the garret and discovered the story book, "Puss in Boots." Yes,

Puss, Junior, felt a little bit homesick, for "no matter how humble, there's no place like home."

Taking Tom Thumb by the hand, he followed the Welsh-woman up the stairs, where they found Taffy sitting propped up in bed, his head done up in great bandages. But, oh, what pleasant blue eyes he had! And his red beard, big and soft, flowed down over the counterpane, and his big strong hand lay so quietly on his lap that Puss forgot he was Puss in Boots, Junior, son of the Seneschal to my Lord of Carabas, and jumped right up on the bed and nestled up to Taffy, purring away just like an ordinary cat!

And what did Taffy do? Did he say "Scat! You'll get the counterpane all dirty with your red-topped boots!" No, he didn't. He just stroked Puss, Junior, with his big, kind hand, and the little Welshwoman picked up Tom Thumb and cuddled him in her bosom, saying in a low voice, "Dearie me, but it's nice to have friends come to see you when everybody in town is calling my Taffy a thief."

And then a tear fell from her eye on little Tom Thumb's hat; but he didn't care, for somehow he felt there must be some mistake, and that Taffy wasn't to blame. And Puss felt the same way, for he kept on purring and rubbing his nose against Taffy's big red hand.

THE RED BEARD

BY and by Taffy stopped stroking Puss, Junior, and said in a kindly voice:

"Well, my fine little cat, what can I do for you?"

Puss, Junior, didn't know just what to answer. In fact, as he hadn't come for anything, he couldn't think of anything to fit the question. But little Tom Thumb, however, called over from where he was sitting in the Welshwoman's lap, that they had come to call, and that they were strangers in town, traveling through on a journey of adventure.

"Did you hear what they say about me?" asked Taffy.

"Yes, we did," replied Puss, "but, somehow, I didn't believe it then; and I'm very sure I don't believe it now."

"Bless you for that," cried the little Welshwoman, "my Taffy is no thief. There has been a great mistake about it all."

"Yes, that there has," said Taffy, "but how can I prove it? Someone with a red beard stole the piece of beef from the butcherman, and then they said it was I. But I was never near his place, nor did I lay hands on meat or marrow-bone."

At that moment there came a loud knocking at the front door, and when the little Welshwoman opened it, whom

should she find but the butcherman himself!

"See what I have brought to you," he said, holding up a false red beard. "I found this to-day behind a barrel in my shop. It's like your Taffy's beard." At this the little Welsh-woman opened her eyes very wide and tried to speak, but she was so surprised she couldn't.

When the butcher went to say that perhaps the man who wore this beard was the one who had stolen his beef, the little Welshwoman began to cry softly, and the big butcher, who had a kind heart, said, "Don't cry, my good woman, I don't think now your Taffy stole the beef, and that's the reason I've come all the way up here to show you this beard. So you tell Taffy that I shall tell everybody in town that it wasn't he who stole my beef, but some thief who wore a red beard: and then, I'll show them what I found in my shop, and that will prove what I say. Everybody will be glad to know that Taffy isn't to blame."

As soon as the butcher had gone, she flew upstairs to tell Taffy the good news. And it almost made Taffy cry. If he hadn't been a man, he would have. But it was hard work not to, just the same. "My head feels better already," he said with a laugh that had a big catch in it.

"Take off the bandages, little woman. I'll come down to supper, and these two small friends of ours shall spend the night with us, for they have brought us good luck to-day, that they have."

ROBINSON CRUSOE

AFTER leaving Taffy, the Welshman, Puss, Junior, and little Tom Thumb walked along for many a mile until they came to the seashore. Right there in a sheltered cove lay a beautiful sailboat, on the stern of which was painted in gold letters:

"Take, oh take me for a sail—

I can weather any gale."

"Shall we accept the pretty boat's offer?" asked Puss, Junior.

For answer Tom Thumb jumped in and, so without another word, Puss hoisted the sail and steered for the big blue ocean. All day and all night they sailed away, and when they woke in the morning they were surprised to find the little boat fast aground on a sandy beach.

"How did we get here?" asked Puss, sleepily, for it was still early in the morning, and the sun had just begun to climb up to the sky, and the dew dripped from the tall meadow grass that grew close to the water's edge.

"Through no fault of ours," replied little Tom Thumb, with a laugh.

"Captain Puss, Junior, fell asleep at the helm, and the first mate, Tom Thumb, did likewise," he added, running up to the bow and looking over the land. "Why, it's an island," he called out. "I can see water on the other side."

"You don't say so," said Puss. "Well, let's land." So they jumped ashore and walked up the beach towards a clump of trees.

"Pretty nice sort of a place," said Tom Thumb. "Let's play Robinson Crusoe! I'll be your black man Friday. We can build a house under these trees, and as we have lots to eat on board ship, we can spend some time here without danger of starving."

And just then, all of a sudden, a voice began to sing:

"Poor old Robinson Crusoe!

Poor old Robinson Crusoe!

They made him a coat

Of an old Nanny Goat;

I wonder how they could do so!

With a ring-a-ting, tang,

And a ring-a-ting, tang,

Poor old Robinson Crusoe!"

"Who's that?" whispered Puss, Junior. But he needn't have asked the question, for just then a man dressed all in skins came toward them.

"Friends or enemies?" he asked.

"Friends!" cried Puss, Junior.

"Friends!" screamed Tom Thumb.

"Welcome, then, to my island. I am Robinson Crusoe!"

Puss and Tom were too amazed to answer for a few minutes. Then Puss, Junior, stretched out his right paw, saying: "I'm very pleased to meet you, Mr. Crusoe."

"And so am I," said little Tom Thumb, standing on tiptoe and reaching up his hand.

"Well, you're certainly as welcome as the flowers in May," said Robinson Crusoe. "Visitors are few and far between. Come with me to my house."

CRUSOE CASTLE

ROBINSON CRUSOE'S home was unlike anything Puss, Junior, had ever seen. Notwithstanding that he had visited many strange places and met many strange people, he was greatly surprised at Robinson Crusoe's style of dwelling. It wasn't exactly like a fort, and yet it was one. Tom Thumb said it reminded him of some of the strange castles he had seen while with Good King Arthur.

It stood against the side of a small hill, surrounded by a high stockade. There was no door to it, but while Puss was wondering how they were going to get in, Robinson Crusoe placed a ladder against the wall and climbed up, saying, "Follow me, my friends; this is the way we enter Crusoe Castle."

After reaching the top they descended by the same ladder, which, of course, was pulled up and lowered on the inside. A very nice looking tent met their eyes, back of which was a large cave hollowed out of the rocky hill.

"Here is where I live, my little friends," cried Robinson Crusoe. "This is my dog, Snoozer, and my two cats, Caromel and Caroline."

Puss had never been very fond of dogs, but Snoozer

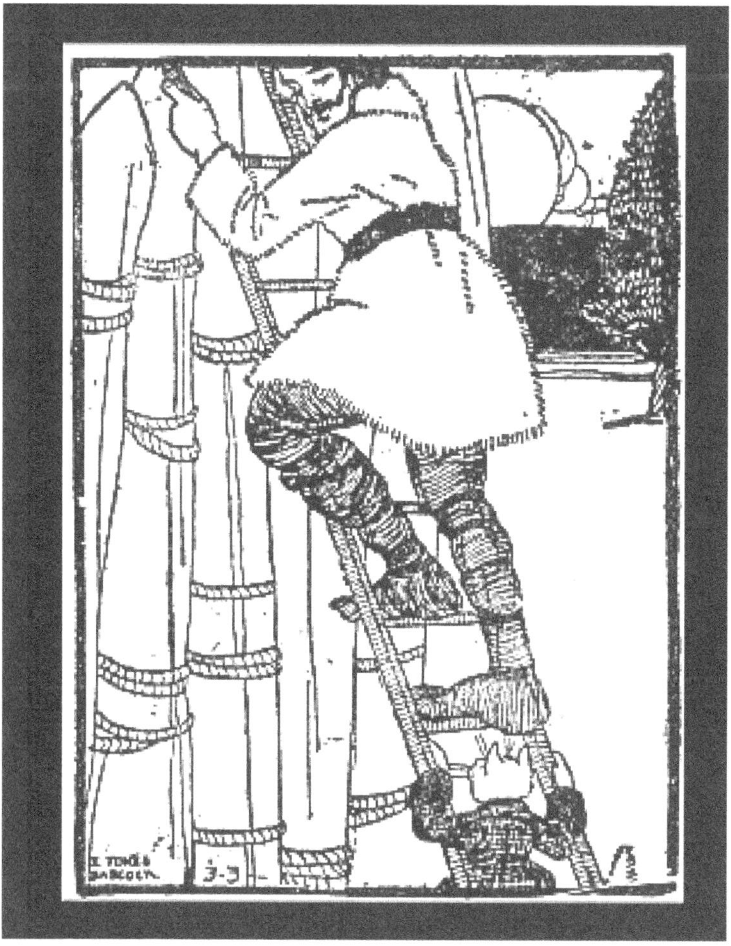

came forward in such a respectful way that Puss took a liking to him at once. I suppose there were so few visitors at Crusoe Castle that Snoozer would have welcomed even a strange cat.

With Caromel and Caroline, however, matters were different. Caromel from the first was jealous of Puss. You see, he had no fine, red-topped boots, nor a sword and feathered cap. Caroline, however, made up for him. She thought Puss, Junior, just about the handsomest cat she had ever seen. Poor Caroline! She had never been off of Crusoe Island.

For all that, however, I don't think if she had been all over the wide, wide world she would have met such a handsome cat as Puss, Junior. No, indeed! Puss, Junior, was the Prince of Cats; that goes without saying, though we have said it.

"And now that we have all been introduced, let us sit down and talk," cried Robinson Crusoe, "for I've hardly spoken to a soul for many years. I've forgotten how a voice sounds."

So they all began to talk and laugh and to tell all sorts of jokes and riddles until it began to grow dark. Then Robinson Crusoe jumped up and said, "Come and watch me get supper, for I am Lord and Chief Cook of Crusoe Castle."

FRIDAY

PUSS, JUNIOR, and Tom Thumb enjoyed their supper at Crusoe Castle better than any meal they ever had. "Even when I visited the Man in the Moon, the cheese wasn't as good as this," said Puss.

"Glad you like it," said Mr. Crusoe, "I made it myself from goat's milk. I have some fine goats, let me tell you. I made me this coat from an old Nanny goat. Do you wonder how Crusoe could do so?"

"Well, I suppose there are no tailors on Crusoe Island," said Tom Thumb.

"I've never met any," replied Mr. Crusoe with a laugh. "I've never met anybody so far except goats and kids, parrots and monkeys, ducks and drakes, snakes and lizards."

"Where did you get Snoozer and Caromel and Caroline?" asked Puss.

"They came off the ship with me when it was wrecked," said Mr. Crusoe. "That is, I brought them off the next day when I went out on the raft to the wreck. And they've been with me ever since."

"Oh, by the way," Puss, Junior, suddenly exclaimed. "Is Friday here?"

"Oh, yes," cried Tom Thumb, "where is Friday?"

Mr. Crusoe got up and walked over to a tall pole and looked over carefully the notches cut into the wood. "Let me see," he said. "To-day is Thursday. Yes, that's right; Friday will be here to-morrow."

"You've made a mistake, Mr. Crusoe," said Puss, with a laugh.

"Have I," he replied, looking over his wooden calendar carefully a second time.

"I don't mean the day," said Puss. "I mean your man Friday."

"Oh, you mean my black man Friday," said Mr. Crusoe. "Oh, I gave him a holiday. He'll be here to-morrow."

"I'm very anxious to see him," said Tom Thumb.

"He'll be surprised when he sees you, too," said Mr. Crusoe, with a grin. "He's never seen a white man but me."

By this time it was quite dark, so Mr. Crusoe lighted some very nice home-made candles and stuck them here and there in the cave. They gave a very soft light. The waves on the beach murmured gently, and pretty soon Snoozer was snoring and Caromel and Caroline were fast asleep on an old sack in a corner.

"Let us turn in," said Mr. Crusoe, showing Puss and Tom a very comfortable hammock. In a short time everybody was sound asleep and snoring away in Crusoe Cave.

SUPPOSING

THE loud ringing of a bell awoke everyone in Crusoe Castle. Puss, Junior, jumped out of his hammock and little Tom Thumb yawned and asked in a sleepy voice, "Who's ringing the door-bell?" Then Mr. Crusoe picked up the ladder and went outside and, placing it against the fence, climbed up to the top, and after that he pulled up the ladder and then let it down on the outside. All this time Snoozer stood below wagging his tail, while Mr. Crusoe's two cats, Caromel and Caroline, purred and rubbed against the calendar pole. Pretty soon a curly-headed black face appeared above the wall.

"Black man Friday," whispered Tom Thumb.

"Bow-wow!" yelped Snoozer, and in a few minutes Mr. Crusoe and his man Friday climbed down the ladder.

"This is my good man Friday," said Mr. Crusoe. So Puss and Tom Thumb shook hands with him, which seemed to please him immensely.

"Glum-glum. Blum-blum!" he cried, smiling and showing a row of very white teeth.

"That's 'Howdy! Pleased to meet you,' in his language," said Mr. Crusoe. "He can talk very little English yet. I've had little time to devote to his education so far."

"But who rang the bell?" asked Puss, Junior.

"Why, Friday did, of course," replied Mr. Crusoe. "Come over here and I'll show you," and he led Puss to the rear of the cave.

"I brought this bell from the wreck," explained Mr. Crusoe. "After Friday came to me I tied a rope to it. At the other end of the rope I fastened a door-knob. When I go out Friday usually stays in. And when I ring the bell he lets down the ladder to me. And when he's out he rings the bell, just as he did this morning, and I let the ladder down to him."

"What do you do when both of you go out?" asked Puss. "Does Snoozer attend to the ladder?"

"No, no," replied Mr. Crusoe. "We hide the ladder in the woods nearby. Then when we come back we get it out and stand it up against the wall and climb up."

"Supposing someone should come across the ladder and make a call while you're out?" asked Tom Thumb.

"Well, I don't know whether they'd think of that if they just happened to find the ladder," answered Mr. Crusoe.

"Well, supposing they did," said Tom Thumb.

"Caesar's Ghost!" cried Mr. Crusoe. "Suppose we don't do any more supposing! I've been so long alone that I've forgotten how to play that game. Let's all go down to the beach and get some fresh soft clams for breakfast. Start the water boiling, Friday, we're going to have steamed clams for breakfast." And then Mr. Crusoe climbed up the ladder, with Puss and Tom Thumb close at his heels.

THREE MEN IN A TUB

ON reaching the seashore, Robinson Crusoe raised a spy glass to his eyes and looked carefully over the water. And then all of a sudden he lowered the glass and whispered: "The cannibals are coming! We must go back to my fort at once."

"Do they eat cats?" asked Puss, Junior.

"I don't know," replied Mr. Crusoe. "You see, I've never met a cannibal; in fact, I've always held aloof from them."

Crusoe's man Friday was nearly frightened to death. He was as pale as a black ghost, which is pretty white for a negro.

Once inside the fort, Mr. Crusoe again took a look at the cannibals. "Why, I guess I've made a mistake," he cried; "it's a tub, not a canoe!"

"Rub-a-dub-dub!

Three men in a tub;

And who do you think they be?

The butcher, the baker,

The candlestick maker,

Turn 'em out knaves all three!"

"Well, that's good news," cried Puss, Junior, while Black Man Friday jumped about in great glee. You see, he had escaped only a short time before from the cannibals.

Little Tom Thumb, although safe inside Puss, Junior's, pocket, was also relieved. The only one who didn't seem overjoyed was Mr. Crusoe himself.

"What's the matter now?" said Puss.

Mr. Crusoe gave a deep sigh. "If you owed the butcher, the baker and the candlestick maker as much as I do you wouldn't be overjoyed at seeing them, either."

"But I'd rather see them than cannibals," cried Tom Thumb. "I'd rather they'd take my money than my life!"

"That's very true," said Mr. Crusoe, "but you don't quite get me. The laws on this island are very strict. They will allow you to shoot a cannibal at sight but not your grocery man."

"Then you are powerless against these three men in a tub?" said Puss, Junior.

"Well, not exactly," replied Mr. Crusoe. "I needn't answer the bell, you know."

By this time the three men had landed on the beach, and pretty soon the doorbell rang.

"S-s-sh!" whispered Mr. Crusoe, "don't make a sound. They can pull the handle off, for all I care."

They didn't do this, but they kept the bell going until every one in Crusoe Castle was nearly crazy. First the butcher took a hand, then the baker, and then the candlestick maker. Then they began all over again.

A BIG FISH

"IF those fellows don't stop ringing that bell, I'll get out my gun," said Robinson Crusoe. "I didn't get the bell for them; it's all paid for long ago."

At that moment, the bell-cord snapped, and the baker, who had just given the handle a dreadful yank, fell over backwards and rolled down the hill to the beach.

"Mr. Crusoe's not at home," said the butcher. "We might as well go back." So he and the candlestick maker went down to the shore and joined the baker; and then all three got into the tub and sailed away.

"And we must do the same," said Puss, Junior. "Tom Thumb and I thank you very much for our nice visit on your island, but it's time we went forth again on our journey of adventure."

"Well, I'm sorry to see you go," said Robinson Crusoe. And after that Puss shoved off the little boat and soon he and Tom were far out of sight on the big, wide sea.

"When the wind is in the East,

'Tis neither good for man nor beast;

When the wind is in the North,

The skilful fisher goes not forth.

When the wind is in the South,

It blows the bait in the fish's mouth;

When the wind is in the West,

Then 'tis at the very best."

"Well, as the wind is in the South, why don't you fish?" cried Captain Puss, Junior. So Tom Thumb started in, and presently he felt a tremendous tug on the line.

"I've got a fish! I've got a fish!" he cried, and then he began pulling in his line as fast as he could. But, oh dear me! It wasn't a fish after all, but a great big whale!

"Don't you pull on that line any more," cried the whale, "if you do I'll smash your boat."

"Oh, is that so," said little Tom Thumb, although, of course, he was frightened almost to death, but what was the use to show fear? It would only make things worse, and if he put on a bold front, perhaps the whale would let them alone.

"I'll take the hook out of your nose, if you'll promise not to swallow me," said little Tom Thumb.

"All right," said the whale, and then Tom tried to pull it out. But it was in so tight that the whale began to spout great big tears. "Oh, dear me! It hurts just like a tooth!"

"Well, it's your own fault!" said Tom. "Next time don't swallow everything that comes along!"

MARY LEE

"IF you're not more careful, I'll spout water over your boat and sink it," cried the whale, growing tired of Tom Thumb's fruitless endeavors to get the fish hook out. "My nose is bleeding now and the hook is still in it."

"Let me give the string a yank," said Tom Thumb. "Didn't you ever have a tooth pulled out that way? It won't hurt much."

"Well, go ahead," said the whale, closing his eyes and shutting his teeth tight. And then out came the hook and over went Tom into the bottom of the boat.

"Ouch! Ouch!" said the whale, while little Tom Thumb picked himself up and said to Puss, Junior, "Don't you ever ask me to fish again in the ocean. I'd rather fish like Simple Simon."

Simple Simon went a-fishing

For to catch a whale;

All the water he had got

Was in his mother's pail.

"What are you grumbling about?" asked the whale, peering over the side of the boat. "One would think you had been caught with a hook," and saying this disagreeable thing, he dived down into the sea.

"No more fishing for me," laughed Tom Thumb.

And just then they came close to a lighthouse on a big rock. So they ran the boat up on the little stretch of sand.

"I don't know what we're landing for," said Captain Puss, Junior, "only I've never been in a lighthouse and here's a good chance."

"Haven't you?" asked a pretty voice, and a young girl appeared on the stone steps leading down to the beach. "Come, my gallant tars, and I'll show you my lighthouse and after that you can tell me some of your adventures, for 'tis a lonely life I lead here alone on the rock until my Bobby Shafto returns."

Bobby Shafto's gone to sea

In his schooner Mary Lee.

Hard-a-port, or hard-a-lee,

"Hasten, Bobby, home to me."

So Puss picked up Tom Thumb and followed the girl into the lighthouse and up the stairs to the very top where the great lamp sent out its rays of light to guide the ships at night; or the great bell clanged in foggy weather to warn the weary sailor from the cruel rocks.

STORY-TELLING

AFTER they had seen everything there was to be seen they all went into the cosy kitchen, Puss, Junior, with Tom Thumb on his shoulder and the pretty girl who kept the lighthouse.

"And now we shall have supper," she said. "And after that, when the lamp is lighted in the tower, we'll sit outside on the doorstep and Puss, Junior, shall tell me one of his adventures."

"Well, what shall I tell and where shall I begin?" asked Puss, when they all were seated outside the lighthouse.

"Tell me how you and Tom became fellow travelers," said the girl, taking Tom up in her hand and placing him on her knee.

"Willingly," said Puss, stroking his whiskers and curling his great mustache, "and should I make a mistake in the telling Tom may correct me.

"When I left my father at the Castle of my Lord of Carabas I had gone but a few miles when I came to Tom Thumb's house. And as soon as his mother saw me she asked me to go to King Arthur's Court and find out about her son, Tom Thumb. She had made him but a few days before a small cambric parasol, and with this as a sort of airship he had floated off on the wind to the castle. When I got there I found that poor Tom was imprisoned in a mousetrap. He had fallen into the dough which the royal baker was about to bake into cakes for King Arthur. And this had so angered the baker that he had thrown Tom into a mousetrap."

"It was worse than that, I was to be beheaded," interposed Tom. "I owe my life to Puss, Junior."

At this, Puss actually blushed, for he was a modest little cat, although he had traveled much and had been royally treated.

"Say not so, my dear Tom," he cried, "for King Arthur was only too glad to comply with my request when I asked him to release you. In fact, it was not because he feared my sword, but because he liked my rhyme."

"How did it run?" asked the girl. And Puss, blushing still more deeply, commenced to recite this little verse:

"My good King Arthur rules this land

With justice and a generous hand.

Far be it that a cat should plead

In vain that Tom Thumb shall be freed."

"Is that what you said?" cried little Tom Thumb. "Dear, dear Puss, I shall never forget what you did for me!"

Dear, dear! Here we are at the end of the book and poor little Puss, Junior, has not yet found his father. Maybe he will in the next book.

THE END